Spyware:

Are You Being Watched?

By John M. Harkins

For the latest information go to:

www. areubeingwatched.com

ISBN-13:978-1466221680

This book is dedicated to my wife Michelle,
I fell in love with her the moment I first saw her.

Table of Contents

Introduction

What is spyware? What is adware? You've probably heard of them because everyone that gets online is either bombarded with information about the products that can help to protect against these two things or get so much spam that they've had to remove it from their system.

Spyware and adware are two separate things but can be lumped together for one reason. That is that they are merciless in what they can do to your computer and to you.

- They risk your sanity with pop up ads.
- They risk your computer too, as too many pieces of adware or spyware on your computer and it will no longer work well.
- And, they will risk your personal identity, too.

www. areubeingwatched.com

Yet, there is much you can do for protection from these problems. The solution is twofold. You must get rid of any type of spyware or adware that is lurking in your computer right now. Then, you need to protect yourself from it entering into your system again.

The information and solutions you need, are within this e-book.

Chapter 1:
Spyware Can Destroy

Spyware and adware are two different animals. Each has the ability to make your life a mess. If you rely on the internet for anything or you rely on your computer for anything, it is a must that you fully understand what these things are and how they work.

The first key to protecting yourself from these things is to fully understand what they are. That will allow you to know how to not make common mistakes that cause spyware to get into your computer.

What Is Spyware?

According to Microsoft, spyware is a term that describes any type of software that is used for such things as collecting personal information, changing the configuration of your computer, advertising and anything else that can be done. The catch is that spyware is downloaded without your permission. Usually, you won't know it's even there when it enters your system.

What Is Adware?

The difference between spyware and adware is just a small one. With spyware, the potential could be leaked personal information to another source. In other words, someone is spying on you. With adware, though, the software is geared towards displaying advertisements.

Is It All Bad?

Unfortunately, many people have been lead to believe that all types of this software are bad and should be avoided. But, that's not always the case. The fact is you may want to have certain types of this software to use.

Remember, to make it spyware it has to be downloaded to your computer without your consent.

Why would you want to have spyware that tracks your personal information? Why would you want those advertisements? You may actually sign up for a service online and when you do you may also agree to receive targeted ads.

Companies like this find it helpful to track where you go online and what you do in order to provide you with ads that are targeted to your interests. Instead of seeing ads that don't have anything to do with you, you'll see ads that are based on the places you've visited online.

In most cases, though, spyware can be something that annoys and even has the potential to do much harm to you and your computer.

www. areubeingwatched.com

Changing Configurations

One problem that often happens with spyware and adware is that they can change your computer's settings, making it quite annoying for you to even log on. Here, they may change the web browser's home page. Or, when you search, this page can be changed. Some products even will make other changes to the actual configuration of your computer.

The problem with these things is that they are usually very difficult to change back. You may not have the ability to do this because it can be quite difficult.

Slowing Your Computer Down

Another problem with spyware and adware is that it can drastically slow your computer down. First and foremost, it can hurt you by being annoying. Pop up ads may happen. But, slowly your computer will begin to move slower. If you don't notice it at first, the more spyware that gets into the system, the harder it will be for you to do the things you want to do.

This happens because your computer is being asked to do more and more. Not only does it need to perform the tasks that you want it to do, but it also needs to perform the tasks that the spyware is running. Running online tracking, popping up ads, monitoring your usage; all of these things can be quite demanding on your system. So, it slows down.

In some cases, so much can be on a computer that it really can stop moving. You may have it crash on you or just go down because it can't perform all of the operations that is being requested of it.

Relaying Information

Some types of spyware are much worse. Although rarer, these are the worst types. Just as adware can track what you are doing online to help target the right ads to you, spyware can do the same.

In some cases, though, it can take pictures of the websites you visit and the information that you input. It may take these images and report them back to the source of the spyware.

When it does that, your personal information, such as your credit card information, your addresses, and even other sensitive information you enter online can be relayed right back to the source.

This is when and why you hear about spyware and adware causing identity theft issues. While these types of situations don't happen as often, they are still potentially there and should be protected from.

The Plan Of Action

Spyware and adware is not something that you can ignore. For most, it is something that needs to on your mind when you are online. Luckily, it doesn't have to be something that you worry about every single day. In fact, there are many ways you can safely protect yourself against these types of problems.

1. **Get your computer clean**. We'll discuss how to do this in the coming

chapters.   Remove all of the adware and spyware on it right now.

2. **Keep it clean**.   Keeping it clean means constant monitoring of what is happening online.   It also means educating yourself in how spyware gets into your computer and protecting yourself from invasion.

Consider spyware and adware as serious as a virus.   Protect yourself and your computer from it.

Chapter 2:
How Does Spyware Spread?

One of the most important things for you to understand is just how spyware spreads. How does it get from its source to your computer?

By understanding this fact, you'll know how to better protect yourself from future invasion.

It's Not A Virus

One thing to know is that spyware and adware are not viruses and don't spread in the same way as a virus would. With a virus, the infected computer system is used to spread the virus from one system to the next. It is actively looking for the next victim. Spyware gets into your system by deception. In most cases, you download it to your computer.

You've Installed It

Most commonly, spyware enters the computer when the computer user installs it. Of course, you wouldn't know that you are doing that. What happens is quite a bit more worrisome.

You visit a website and find a piece of software that you would like to have. You download it. Little did you know that the software that you just downloaded had spyware piggybacked onto it and now you've got both the desirable software and the spyware lurking on your computer. You may not even know it's there for months!

Or, you may have the spyware trick you into downloading it. In this case, you may be asked to perform an operation that is "required" to complete the download. When you do, you are actually downloading the spyware or adware onto your computer.

Some of the newest versions of this software are even more devastating because they promise to protect your computer. You may download a program and it offers security software with its download. You download it thinking it's stopping spyware when in fact it is doing the opposite. It's actually the spyware itself.

In some cases, the spyware gets onto your computer by pretending to offer you a useful service or tool. For example, a common type of spyware "giveaway" is a web accelerator, promising to speed up your interactions online, making surfing the net faster. It's not going to do this for you at all.

Some of these types of programs have even been targeted at children. They may offer a "friend" that gets to monitor what your child does online, keeping them safe and giving them the ability to do things online without your watchful eye.

The problem is he may also be a spyware tool that will target ads directly at your child during those sessions with him.

Shareware

Another way that spyware gets into the computer is through shareware. It often comes bundled with this type of product. One type of this program would be file trading utilities. When you purchase and install the program you want, you also download the spyware.

Some companies that have the need and potential benefits from spyware and adware even have worked with the shareware providers in paying them to incorporate the spyware into the software that you are likely to download and use.

More commonly, shareware gets the spyware bundled into it by the spyware companies.

In these cases, the shareware providers don't know that it is there.

You've Changed Security Features

Unfortunately, there are other ways that spyware and adware can get into your computer. For example, it may be in the form of altering your security features. It may even prompt you to do this without realizing what you are doing.

Internet Explorer's web browser offers built in notifications to the user of when something is trying to download onto your computer or, when something is making a change to your system. But, these can be manipulated with the simple click of a link on a website.

Consider the annoying pop up ad. A pop up ad is one that literally pops up when you are using your computer. Usually they happen when you visit websites. In most cases, just by closing the ad, you are done. But, have you ever fallen for those ads that look very much like Windows security boxes?

These can actually be triggers for spyware to be downloaded. They look an awful lot like a standard dialog box providing you with information. You click on them, they change your security features and within a few minutes, you've got spyware to deal with. That's anything but something you want to have happen.

One such dialog box offers to "optimize your internet access." Even if you hit the "No" button, you've still clicked on the ad, which is enough to push it to download.

Security holes in your system can be another way that spyware gets in. Here, they could be in your webs browser or the holes could be lurking in a program you are using. If you are browsing the web and happen to a location where spyware software like this is lurking, it can actually attack these holes in your system and force the computer to download the software. This is often called a drive by download.

This can happen with both Internet Explorer and with Microsoft Java runtime where security risks lie. Those that have created this type of spyware software have an extensive knowledge of anti virus software and firewall software.

Through A Virus?

While spyware is much different than a virus, spyware can be the actual virus's intention. For example, if a virus like this gets onto your computer it may install tons of spyware at one time to your computer.

This was the case with one type of virus known as W32.spybot.worm. It used pornographic information to infect the user's system and challenged all types of ads because of it.

These are the most common methods in which spyware can get into your computer. Sometimes, you, the computer user are the one to make the decision to download it by downloading another program. Other times, it pushes its way into your computer.

Yet, even as dangerous as these things can be, the fact is that you can keep using the internet and using the downloads you find there.

You just have to learn how to spot potential problems and how to avoid unwanted extra programs.   In effect, you need to also monitor your computer's needs even if you haven't downloaded a thing.

In the coming chapters, we'll discuss the actual methods of removal. Then, we'll come back to learning to protect yourself against downloads that may contain spyware or adware in them.

Chapter 3:
How To Remove Spyware

There are several ways to remove spyware from your computer. If you have knowledge of viruses, then you can easily understand most of these methods and how they are potentially beneficial to you.

Spyware can be detected in many of the same ways as a virus can. A scan of your computer can relieve many types of spyware and adware and help you to safely remove them from your computer.

The worst case scenario for the computer user that has a large amount of spyware and adware on their computer is to have to have their computer's system reinstalled. In this case, it will take professional help, in many cases, to back up the data on the computer and then to fully reinstall the operating system for the unit.

But, that's not the normal case and it's not the first step for you to take, either. There are several other things that you should do first. There is much help out there but it takes a bit more help and knowledge to get you to the point of knowing what program is a potential benefit and which is likely not to be.

It's Gotten Bad

It's important to realize that spyware is no longer something that happens to the other guy. You have to consider this a strong risk as you would a virus. You don't have to make a mistake in downloading it to your computer to be a victim to it. It can just happen.

In that, there are countless products on the market that claim to be able to provide you with the very best resource for removing spyware and adware from your computer.

Some are very much capable while others can even be spyware programs lurking themselves.

It will cost you. If you have no spyware protection on your computer right now, you'll need to invest in it. That could be a decent amount of money to start with. But, if you let it go and have to have your computer's operating system fully reinstalled, that will cost you even more.

Therefore, it makes sense to make decisions now to improve your system.

Three Steps To Removing Spyware

There are three main steps that you will have to fully understand to keep spyware and adware at bay. Without one of these components, you are at a potential risk for allowing it into your computer.

Step 1: Anti Spyware Programs

These programs provide you with the ability to clean up your system. They work much like a virus program in that they will remove anything hidden on your computer that could potentially be risky for you.

They also provide protection such as a firewall that will help to prevent further infestations of spyware on your computer after it has been successfully removed.

Step 2: Beware Of What's Out There

You need to know which programs have the most potential for hurting you. There are many programs that are commonly used and have spyware or adware lurking in them. We'll show you which ones are potential risky investments.

Step 3: Be Secure

There are specific security measures that you must put in place to provide protection against future invasions of spyware. These methods will offer you a strong protection against making mistakes or even allowing holes in your security system to put you at risk.

By explaining to you what options you have, you'll have the ability to make the right decision about the right protection for spyware and adware for you.

There is no doubt that you should be careful when you are online to avoid potentially problematic spyware or adware situations. Nevertheless, it will be very difficult to protect yourself 100% of the time. Yet, with a few simple measures, you can find be vigilant in defying the odds against spyware.

Finally, it is important to make mention of the fact that any type of education that you receive on spyware and adware should be communicated to the whole family, or at least anyone that uses your computer. Children can often be targets of spyware and adware. Remember that all it takes is a click of the mouse to download it.

Educating your children on this potential threat will help you to find true benefit in the effectiveness of the program. Most children that can use the computer on their own can understand what potential security risks are in place. Give them a checklist to protecting themselves and your computer investment.

Chapter 4:
Anti Spyware Programs

Anti spyware programs are going to be the most effective and beneficial tool for you to use in your fight against all things spyware. In most cases, it will remove most of the spyware and adware from your computer.

Some types of spyware can pose a larger problem and often be difficult to remove. Nevertheless, there are some excellent tools available to help most computer users to combat the threat of spyware.

Programs Available

There are many programs on the market that can be helpful in removing spyware. While we are not advocating for any one program here, there are several that must be mentioned in order to learn what these are, what they can do and just where they came from.

One such program is that of OptOut. This program was designed by Steve Gibson and really became one of the founding tools in the fight against spyware. It was one of the first tools to do this and therefore was the foundation for other programs that were to come along.

Some of the most popular tools include Ad-Aware which was designed by Lavasoft. Another program is that of Spybot-Search and Destroy which was created by Patrick Kolla.

These programs have helped many to fight. In fact, they not only removed spyware but they worked at helping to stop the download of them, too.

You can also look at Microsoft for some help. Just months ago, they began working on a program to help with this type of protection. The program was for Windows XP, Windows 2000 or Windows 2003, and was a free downloadable program that expired in July in its beta version. It was called Windows AntiSpyware beta.

The second version of this program is called Windows Defender and is a second beta test. This one is available through the end of 2006. While this program is available, it may be worth your time to use to protect your computer. It is expected that a full version will be available in 2007 after the beta test has been completed.

Still, there are many more anti spyware programs available to fill your needs. Which one is the right choice for you? There's still much to take into consideration.

How About A Free One?

One thing you may be tempted by is a free anti spyware program. Free programs seem quite alluring after all, no one really wants to have to pay for protection if it is available without charge.

When considering free anti spyware products, take the time to truly unearth who they are, what they offer and what they put onto your computer. There are some excellent free programs to consider.

Yet, there are many more that are quite likely to contain spyware or adware themselves and be a simply ploy to get you to download them. Therefore, unless you've done your research on the product, something we'll talk more about in a few minutes, don't download anything.

Anti Spyware And Virus Protection

One of the many things you'll find today in spyware protection are those programs that are now coupling anti virus products with anti spyware products. Each of them can be beneficial.

Some of the companies that have begun putting these together include McAfee, Symantec and Sophos. These leading anti virus software protectors are now providing software that will handle spyware at the same time as virus protection.

But, did you know that not all of these programs were really interested in doing this? While from a customer standpoint you can easily see how spyware is just as dangerous as viruses, from the business point, there was concern.

What if an anti spyware program labeled a company's product as spyware? Could they be sued for doing so? These are real concerns to this day for these software developers as you can understand.

Most of them have simply labeled programs that they consider to be possible spyware programs with a term that is less offensive such as Symantec's use of "extended threats" during a scan of your computer.

Should you purchase the combination of these two very important tools for your computer? It is a personal decision which program you do use and/or purchase. But the fact is that you must have something working for you to provide you with ultimate protection.

It's understandable for most to be confused by which program is the right one to work with. Some people seem to think more than one program is necessary. Yet, an up to date program is the perfect choice.

How They'll Aid You

No matter if you've actually gotten to the point of selecting a product yet or not, you do need to realize how they will work for you. There are two concepts to understand in anti spyware programs.

First of all, just as a virus program would run a "scan" on your computer, a spyware program will do about the same. It will run through the files on your computer, in most cases both obvious files and hidden files.

When it spots something that has the potential of being spyware, it collects its location and details. After the scan is complete, it will provide you with details on what was found, where it was located and what it is.

In some cases, you'll be able to remove the program fully from your computer. In other cases, it is necessary for you to just block the files from working as they've placed themselves in such a place or manner that they can't be easily removed.

Most programs will run checks on these areas if not more while running a scan:

- Your Window's registry
- Your operating system files
- Files that you've installed through programs

The second way in which anti spyware programs work is by providing protection to you. Go back to your virus program. It protects you by providing you with a real time protection.

If a virus was to try and enter your computer while you are using it and you have a running anti virus program, it captures the virus and stops it from entering.

Anti spyware works in just about the same manner as anti virus does. If a program attempts to download something to your computer and it doesn't have the necessary allowance for doing so, your running, real time anti spyware program stops it and asks you if you wanted that program to be downloaded. If you don't you tell the program to stop it. If you do, then you allow it.

During this process it will update you, providing you with the necessary information to make a decision about the program trying to get in. It may give a full description of the program and give you advice as to what to do with it.

It works quite simply by taking the time to scan through the incoming network data and disk files. Before these are able to be fully downloaded, they get a full scan at the download time, before it hits your computer.

How does it know if a program is spyware? In most cases, it will stop anything that looks suspicious. In addition to this, most have a working list of "known to represent spyware" programs. It doesn't remove these from your system, but stops the download of something suspicious.

At that point, you make the decision to continue with the program download or stop it.

One thing to consider in an anti spyware program is a program that allows the interception of programs that are trying to install start up items. They may also offer protection from those programs that are trying to modify your browser settings in some way. Using this is helpful as many spyware and adware programs take advantage of browser weaknesses.

This software is often marketed as security software. Don't assume that your anti spyware program does this, though, as it is quite possible that it will not.

The combination of these two things allows your computer system to stay protected: on going, real time protection and detection and removal programs.

What's On The Market

A common misconception today is that any anti spyware and anti adware program on the market provides the same types of protection and constant coverage. This is not the case, unfortunately.

Some programs are still just providing detection and removal applications to the user. Javacool Software produced the first product that would offer coverage in real time protection.

Their product is called Spyware Blaster. In fact, they were the first to successfully provide help for the spyware program known as ActiveX based spyware, a large threat. Today, this program offers comprehensive coverage in the realm of protection and prevention.

Yet, it can be much more beneficial to find a program that will offer you both real time protection as well as removal and detection tools. Look for a anti spyware program that pulls these resources together to provide the most complete coverage against spyware programs and adware programs alike.

Installing Isn't Enough

Once you've found and installed your program, you're done, right?

You can't just download your program and forget all about it, assuming that it is protecting you. Like virus programs, anti spyware and anti adware programs also need to be updated.

Just as your virus protection requires updating because the world of viruses change, so does the world of spyware. Without an up to date definition of the program, you are still just as exposed as when you didn't have any anti spyware software.

Why do you need to do this? It's simple. Spyware developers, good or bad as they are, are constantly looking for a new way to present their software in order to work, rather than becoming trapped in an anti spyware product. They are looking at how they can get around it, so to speak.

The good thing is that anti spyware program designers are doing the same thing. When a new type of strain of spyware becomes evident to them, they develop tools to stop it through the software programs they have in place.

The program is discovered and then evaluated. Once it is fully understood, the developer creates a unique signature or definition for that specific new threat.

Once this update has been added to your computer's anti spyware protection through an update, your computer is once again, fully protected. Without these, your computer is still quite at risk for further or future spyware and adware invasions.

www. areubeingwatched.com

How To Get Updated Protection

To get this up to date protection, you'll need to know just how your anti spyware protection works. Each program is a bit different. Yours might be one of these types of programs or another. does

- If the program is a subscription, that is paid for in order to get services over a period of time, these programs are often updated throughout that time period of subscription.

- If the program is a one time download or scan, you'll need to manually make the update happen. That may mean downloaded a new scan for each time you use it.

In most cases, the updates will come as part of the price of the subscription to the anti spyware, anti adware program. In fact, this is the best choice as it will provide the most frequent updates. Most of the time, these can be set up to do this type of updating automatically whenever the computer is connected to the internet and there is an update available.

If this is not the case, a schedule of updates may be followed. During this type of situation, a schedule is set in which during certain intervals the updates will be downloaded automatically from the anti spyware provider.

If you are visiting a website and doing a scan that is manual, the program will look for and provide any updates before the scan is actually run.

Finally, some programs require manual updating. That means you'll need to visit the website, download the updates and then run a scan after doing so to remove anything and everything that was covered in the update.

Want No Updates?

There are programs available that don't require actual updates. Instead, they will use historical observation as their method of defining and stopping spyware. These programs can do this fully or partially. To work, they'll monitor specific configuration parameters. This includes areas of your Window's registry and your browser.

When there is any change to these aspects of your computer, it will alert you to it. As the user, you can then decide if the change is supposed to happen, or if it is wanted.

At that point, you, as the user has to make a decision about whether or not this is the right program for you to delete or one that you should have.

The good thing about them is that you don't have to worry about getting updates for this software. Instead of relying on that, it relies on what's on your computer currently and changes that are made.

The problem with this type of anti spyware and anti adware program is that most don't know which files and downloads are potentially harmful and which are innocent enough. The program doesn't offer any type of recommendation to you, nor does it offer any type of judgment to contain the file change.

With some of these programs, you can use a community based resource available to you. With that, you can determine what the right action is by visiting the community, finding out what others did and their success and then making your decision based on this information provided.

This type of set up is also quite useful to those that are monitoring and analyzing spyware as they can see what potential problems are flowing throughout the web at any given time and with what type of frequency it is happening.

The Un-Removable

Even with some of the best anti spyware and anti adware programs, it is quite possible that some spyware on your computer won't come off. There are several types of programs that keep themselves in the loop.

- This type of spyware often resists your attempts to find, uninstall or destroy it.

- It can often work with another program (two spyware programs that are separate but often downloaded at the same time.) When it does this, you'll attempt to destroy it but the other spyware program kicks in when this happens and re-spawns the other spyware, causing it to be fully functional.

- It may also work with its own programming. When it figures out that the anti spyware program has removed registry keys, it may quick reinstall them.

So, how can you safely and complete get rid of these seemingly impossible to remove spyware programs?

One solution is to load the computer in safe mode. Doing this, and then running your anti spyware program will allow for more success. .

Even still, there are additional problems that can still be resisting. For example, a somewhat new type of spyware is working so well at hiding inside your systems critical process. These programs can often run even when you boot your computer in safe mode. These are difficult to removal as well as detect.

Even worse, some spyware and adware programs are so well designed that they don't leave any type of on disk signature on your computer, making them near impossible to locate.

One program, known as Gromozon, is a spyware program that has the capability of even blocking anti spyware programs from being installed into your computer or allowing them to run there.

It is also possible that the spyware will need to be tackled by a professional team that has complex methods of detecting and removing spyware and adware that is resisting other methods of removal. This is especially true when quite a bit of spyware is found on a computer.

As mentioned earlier, there are some computers that are so infected or that have nearly impossible spyware or adware programs running in it that the entire operating system will need to be reinstalled. Although this is rare, it is still a possible need you may have.

All of this information about anti spyware programs is critical for you to fully understand. Because there are so many beneficial programs out there, it is essential for you to know which the best possible product is for you.

It is also important to realize that not all programs offered are the best possible choice. In fact, some programs are anything but.

Finding an anti spyware and anti adware program for your use should be a well researched project. You'll need to take the time to fully learn about the product.

In the next chapter, we will reveal some of the worst case scenarios.

Chapter 5:
The Anti Anti-Spyware Programs

Unfortunately for the common pc user, there are some pretty awful companies out there that like to deceive. The good news is that most of these companies are well known for the types of anti spyware products they put on the market.

If you are educated about these programs, you won't fall victim to them.

As we mentioned earlier, there are some anti spyware programs established that actually are anything but safe programs to use. Some are actually spyware themselves, which means that you will download something you think will help and benefit your computer use only to find out that they can't do anything of the sort.

There are several ways in which this type of spyware program can be used against you. They are nothing more than fake anti spyware programs.

How It Can Happen To You

There are several ways that this type of spyware can make it onto your computer. For starters, you'll want to monitor the pop up ads that you respond to offered throughout the web.

We've already talked about how potentially dangerous they are. But, even when they seem to be anything but dangerous or may seem to be helpful, they are anything but.

Some of these fake anti spyware and adware programs used banner ads all over the web.

You clicked on those ads and within a few seconds you were directed to another website which encouraged you to purchase programs that were anti spyware or anti adware programs. The problem is that they weren't.

- In some cases, they were just other programs that took a couple of dollars from your pocket claiming to be offering you some sort of protection.

- Then, there were other types that actually were promising to provide your computer with anti virus protection.

- Some used promises of protection against spyware and adware, claiming to be a full fledge software application for protection.

- Others claimed to be registry cleaners that would offer a service to you.

All of these spyware programs can be lumped together under the term "rogue software," as they are commonly called.

Some of these programs were able to lure a person into downloading them. Others were actually designed to install just through a few clicks through a website.

To help you to get the protection you need, we've listed some of the worst of these anti anti-spyware programs here. You can find more information about any of these programs online.

Most of them have been disabled and many of the better anti spyware and anti adware programs have updated definitions to protect against these programs. Some do not, though.

Anti Spyware To Avoid:

- VirusBlast
- Spyware Quake
- SpywareStrike
- Pest Trap
- The Shield 2006
- Mallware
- SpyBan
- PSGuard
- PAL Spyware Remover
- Spyware Stormer
- Brave Sentry
- AntispywareSolider
- AlfaCleaner
- Privacy Defender
- PSGuard
- SpyWiper
- SpyTrooper
- SpyFalcon
- WorldAntiSpy
- WinFixer
- Malware Wipe
- SpyAxe

Some of these programs have had legal action taken against them. In fact, in early 2006, Microsoft and the Washington State Attorney General secured a lawsuit against the company Secure Computer.

The company was producing a product that was supposed to be a Spyware Cleaner, which actually was anything but. The state has in fact spyware laws that make spyware a legal process in the state. The State and Microsoft won their battle in this case.

As a consumer, it is quite worrisome when you are looking for a good anti spyware program. After all, if there are so many different types of programs available that promise to benefit you only to lead you in the other direction.

There is something you can do. If you still aren't sure which the right anti spyware program is for you, or you want more information, the best decision to make is to learn.

You want to learn about your options. Take your time in finding several programs to consider. Don't just download whatever you find. Make sure that the program that you do download is one that you know you can trust.

Chapter 6:
Research And Learn More

Does everyone hate that word, research?

Don't worry, this isn't a complicated process.

If you are looking for an anti spyware or anti adware product, do your research. The fact is that through a bit of research you'll find the best possible program for your needs and not get taken by something that does more harm to your computer then it will do good to your computer.

Get Started

Take a few minutes to find several programs that interest you. Remember, you'll want to pay attention to the details. The best possible choice is a program that will detect and remove spyware but also features real time monitoring of your computer to stop spyware from being downloaded in the process.

So, your first task is to look for several programs to learn more about. Even if you think you know the provider, you should learn more about the actual anti spyware program before going on.

Learn About Them

With a list in hand, you'll want to do some investigating. Here is a list of things that you must learn before you can choose the right anti spyware program.

1. **Who makes the program?** This information is available when you purchase the product. Obviously, if you know Microsoft makes something, you know the company. Yet, there are plenty of great tools out there for anti spyware that are not associated with

well known brand names. Therefore, don't assume that well known brands are the best choice for you.

2. **Who is the manufacturer, really?** Take some time to do some research on the manufacturer. Do they provide other software products? Do a search for them. What do you learn? Even better, what can you find about the company's history? The more you can uncover about the manufacturer, the better.

3. **Visit the website of the Better Business Bureau.** Look for both the product name and the company that manufacture's it. There, you'll learn if there are any complaints about the product or company that have gone unresolved. Not all companies will be listed, there, though. Nevertheless, learning the company's rating at the

BBB is a good step and decision to make now.

4. **Look for software reviews.** Many websites provide detailed reviews that are left by consumers that have used the product in the past. You may be one of these after you select and use the anti spyware product of your choice. You can often use their information to make the right decision.

5. **Visit forums and message boards to learn more.** Just a search for anti spyware programs online will lead you to many discussions. That's because it is such a large topic with lots of resources. You can learn what others are using as well as get expert advice about one product or the other.

It really does pay to use other's experiences to help you to make the right decision about your own product. There are countless times, though, when you can make this decision on your own. What you should know is that using anti spyware and anti adware doesn't have to be a decision that you make and never change your mind about.

Chapter 7:
Choosing The Best Anti Spyware Tool

The bottom line is, "Which is the best possible anti spyware tool for me?"

The answer is complex. There are several things to take into consideration now that you've done all of the necessary research to learn about the spyware options you have. Take in all of this before you make a decision, though.

More Than One

One thing to consider is to have several anti spyware tools available to you to use. Here's the thing. There are some good free anti spyware products out there. After you've done your research and know which ones are acceptable, it can be helpful to pair several together.

Why do you need more than one? As we've mentioned, definitions and updates change. Some may have more advanced or even more specific solutions than others do. Some may look in other files than others. Some are more selective while others are more complete.

Pairing a couple of programs together can often help you to find the best solution. If you do go this route, make sure that you've done your homework. You want to make sure that any product your download is actually clean of spyware itself.

If you do this, you'll also want to be selective in which programs you choose for cost reasons. It would be pretty expensive to download three or four programs that cost $50 each. Instead, look for high quality lower costing products and pair them together.

This is also a good way to get more for the money you plan to invest in this search for anti spyware products.

Having more than one product can be helpful, but let's first plan on getting just the first one done so that you can start protecting your computer.

Find The Experts

There are some excellent webmasters and bloggers available that take the time to meticulously download, run and then review software tools. This is an excellent tool for you to use. They usually offer their services without cost with the sole purpose of educating you.

To find these authors, just do a Google search for spyware bloggers. Then, visit their website and sign up for their newsletters or their RSS feed. Why bother doing this? It's simple. They review products that are available to you. They take the time to do all of the comparison work for you.

It's a great way to learn more about what's out there and to be able to compare one anti spyware program to the next, in black and white.

When you visit these websites, many of the bloggers or webmasters actually provide a reviewing system for the consumer. Find one or two of the best rated anti spyware products.

Even better is to visit several of these websites and get a good idea about which ones are the very best overall. The ones recommended by several are even better.

One thing to consider about these, though, is that these reviewers shouldn't be making a commission from selling one or the other product. Look for an honest reviewer to take advantage of.

Make this part of your decision process. It gives you not only information about your options but also the expert advice you need.

Price

Let's face it, cost matters to most of us no matter what the benefit of a computer protection level is. Cost should play a role in the type of anti spyware product you purchase.

Remember this rule: Not all free anti spyware products are okay to use. But, the most expensive anti spyware products are likely to be no better than another other product.

You are looking for something in the middle. Here's what you want to consider in relation to the cost of any anti spyware protection tool.

What does the program offer in the way of protection?

In price consideration, it may be cheaper to use a detection and removal tool that can be found right online without cost. But, what you truly need is a tool that will take this to the next step. That is, it needs to protect you in real time, as we've discussed.

If it does not provide this, it is likely to cost you much less. But, if you can't remember to weekly (or more often) visit the location and run the spyware, you are in a potentially risky situation. If you can count on running that type of a check often, then this low cost may be beneficial.

How Do You Get Upgrades?

The next important consideration is what type of updates you can get. If you subscribe to a service, you may be able to save yourself some money in getting updated signatures and definitions for the anti spyware program you install.

We've talked about how programs are updated and why, but the question is, how does this effect your cost of the program. Of course, a program that provides constant monitoring is going to be more costly. But, the updates on these programs usually happen as they are available. Other programs will need you to visit manually to make them happen.

Since most people would have a hard time remembering to visit and get the necessary upgrades, you'll want to carefully consider how this will affect your specific needs.

It may be worth paying a bit more for the protection of updates that happen automatically. That way, your computer is protected against constant spyware threats. There is no doubt that you need to have these downloaded to the software tool you are using. Don't skimp on this as an old, or un-updated or under- updated product is useless.

Is It Part Of A Bundle?

Some anti spyware and anti adware products are actually more affordable if you purchase them with other software products that you need.

For example, you may find that your Internet Service Provider may provide a free spyware and adware scan as part of your subscription to their service.

If you choose to use a program like this, spend a few minutes looking at who the company is and what type of quality the product actually has. Many of the leading ISP's are now offering this as an additional service.

Is it cheaper, though? Often, you can combine the anti spyware and anti adware products you are selecting along with anti virus products. This can be quite rewarding if you are looking for both tools. You definitely need to have these on your system.

As we mentioned, McAfee and Symantec are bundling these services together, which means that you may be able to save a great deal of money on them if you purchase them together.

Whenever you consider bundling any type of software together, learn all about what you're getting and the quality of each element.

There are plenty of times when this won't be a good idea and plenty of times where it can be a great tool.

Take The Trial

The last suggestion for this section that we have for you allows you to get the best possible benefit for your money. That is to use the free trial run.

Before you actual do this, though, take the time to really learn about the company. A free trial version of a software product is great as long as it doesn't have its own versions of spyware to download onto your computer.

Again, do your homework and find out more about the company first and their product. Look for information about what others have experienced. Then, when all checks out, take the free trial version.

When you do this, you'll be able to see several things. First off, you can see how the software works. Is this what you wanted? Or, is it too hard to manage? You can also learn more about the features that are available (or that aren't available.) Getting a real picture of what is offered is important here.

The trial version is likely to be only offered for a limited time and may even be something that offers limited coverage. Here's what you should do during that time.

- Find all features and give them a try. Do you like them?
- Take the time to run scans on your computer. Note the found potentially harmful spyware on your computer. Do remove them. Then, run another scan by another program altogether. Did it

come close to getting all the possibly infected files?

- Find out costs for subscribing and what they include.
- Use customer service for something to learn how useful they are.
- Compare two or three programs like this to see which the best choice is for your needs and your preferences in protection.

A free trial is a great way to learn more about the product you are buying. If a company doesn't offer one, wonder why and then avoid them. Wouldn't they want to show off their product?

Chapter 8:
Computer Security And Spyware

As we mentioned earlier, there are different aspects to managing spyware.

1. The first of those is to have a good anti spyware product to use.
2. The second was to avoid programs that are potentially damaging. For this one, we'll give you a list in the next chapter.
3. The third thing to consider is that of your computer security.

Your computer is capable of offering some protection against spyware and just trouble in general. But, for that to happen, you need to do a little learning yourself to learn how to provide the necessary protection.

Here, we'll provide you with some things you can do to increase your computer's security.

Each of these things is something you should consider using.

Your Web Browser

The first thing to take a look at is the type of web browser you are using. Internet Explorer is one of the most targeted spyware and adware browsers. That's because of a number of different factors, especially the fact that there are security holes in many of the products.

Some people will use a different web browser other than Internet Explorer. Some of the ideal choices include Mozilla Firefox and Opera.

Why are these any better than others? The fact is that they really aren't, but they are not targeted nearly as much as Internet

Explorer users are targeted by spyware programs.

Firewalls

Another solution to improve the security of your computer is to install and use firewalls. If you've ever used a computer at your college or university (or most businesses are now using them) then you know what we're talking about.

Firewalls (as well as web proxies) help to keep users of the internet from visiting websites that are known for being hazardous in the way of spyware and adware.

The firewall works because it just blocks the user from visiting websites that are known to be spyware laden. BY doing this, the user is less likely to actually download the spyware to their computer.

You can get a firewall easily. Many internet service providers are now offering them as part of their security.

Shareware Protection

Computer security can also be helpful when the user knows what's happening. By taking the time to avoid using programs that are shareware, or choosing programs that are not laden with spyware, is also helpful.

Some shareware providers are now offering the ability to protect yourself by having all programs researched and cleared of being possible spyware or adware. One example is CNet which is monitoring which files it keeps in its directory, to provide only safe downloads to its customers.

Your computer's security is an important consideration when it comes to spyware and adware. Take the time to make sure that if your computer needs to be updated with protection that you make sure that it happens.

Chapter 9:
The Programs To Avoid

There are plenty of times when you will go to download a specific program that is completely necessary only to find out that the download also comes with a host of spyware and adware.

It's unfortunate that this happens, but it does. When it does happen, you'll need to make a decision about the product and whether or not it is the right choice for your specific needs.

We mentioned in the beginning that this some spyware wasn't necessarily bad and that it may be something you even agree to download and have on your computer in order to get the software you really want. In that case, it might not even be a bad ideal.

Still, you'll need to make sure that you avoid any program that isn't necessary that has potentially damaging spyware and adware components to it. If a program has spyware on it, you should also know about it.

That's what we'll do here.

Software Products Known To Have Spyware

Good or bad, here's a list of software products you may download that are known to contain spyware and/or adware with them.

- Kazaa
- Dope Wars
- WeatherBug
- EDonkey2000
- ErrorGuard
- Bonzi Buddy
- FlashGet
- Morpheus
- RadLight
- Grokster

Messenger Plus! is another software program that is often downloaded with spyware, but this is only done if you actually agree to install what they call their sponsor program.

There are a number of different programs that have in the past had spyware and/or adware with their download. This includes AOL Instant Messenger, LimeWire, WIldTangent, and DivX.

Chapter 10:
Is It Legal?

A common question that is asked is whether spyware and adware is actually legal. The fact is that in most cases the answer is, no, its not. But, that doesn't always stop all crime.

What is illegal is being able to get into anyone's computer without their authorization for any reason. In the United States, the law that covers this is the Computer Fraud and Abuse Act.

Since part of the definition of spyware and adware is that the process itself requires that a user download the program without the knowledge and/or consent of the user then it is quite illegal in itself. It is a tricky law, though, that is very open to consideration.

It is so difficult to prosecute those that make and distribute spyware and adware that it is, in fact, something rarely done. In some cases, many of these companies operate as standard businesses. It's not a hidden trade in any way, in many situations.

Why is it so difficult? One of the reasons this is the case is the fact that they have to prove that you didn't want to download the software in the first place.

Let's say that you were using shareware and the process included spyware. Some spyware providers claim that you signed up for the spyware as part of the bundle of applications.

Another consideration is just how you give your consent. Be honest, how many times have you read through those long, "Read me" agreements before purchasing or downloading some type of software?

If you don't read the End User License Agreement, as they are called, and click "yes, you agree" and continue, guess who's legally responsible for whatever happens?

To make this even worse, many of the spyware and adware companies will make these agreements excessively long and difficult to read and understand. You get frustrated and just hit that button.

Of course, in most cases of spyware and adware, there is no agreement to sign anyway. The fact is that many of these are drive by downloads that you'll never know the program is there. In this case, there is no contract at all and therefore nothing to hold you to them.

The good news is that throughout the United States and in countries such as Australia, there is much law making happening to provide some protection from spyware and adware to the public.

In Iowa and Washington, within the United States, there have been laws passed that offer some protection. In these laws, specific types of spyware are targeted and made to be criminalizing acts.

In most cases, the target is any type of software that changes web browser settings, that disables any computer security tools or that monitors the keystrokes you use.

Unfortunately, for many types of spyware and adware, the laws aren't in place to offer you the protection you need. Or, they are so difficult to prosecute and track that there is little that you can do on that front.

The only suggestion that can be made in this situation is that you, as a citizen, encourage your legislators to work on protecting your identity and your investments by issuing anti spyware and adware laws.

Until then, you'll have to protect yourself.

www. areubeingwatched.com

Chapter 11:
Checklist Of Protection

Now that you know all that you need to know about spyware and adware, its time to get your computer and all computers you use safe. Here's a checklist to help you to make that happen.

1. Find the right anti spyware protection software by doing research. Look for a program that detects, removes and provides real time protection against the installation of spyware.

2. Educate your family on how to be safe online from not only viruses but also from spyware and adware traps.

3. Get your updates. Once you have software installed, get the updated definitions regularly.

4. Run scans. Set up your software to run a scan of your computer daily (if you are online constantly) or weekly. Monitor what is found and block or remove it from the computer.

5. Keep up to date. Keeping yourself up to date on the information that is available and the latest worrisome trends is part of the process of keeping yourself safe.

Conclusion

Are you worried about your computer and spyware? If not, then reread this e-book. The fact is that spyware is a problematic, unwanted and often disruptive type of software that can cause untold damage on a computer or even on your identity.

While the type of spyware that steals the identity of individuals is much less common, the other types of spyware are very common and very much something that you should be concerned with.

Take the steps necessary to fight your battle against spyware. Yet, it can be very simple and even something you don't have to think about. The best bet is to purchase an all inclusive anti spyware, anti adware program that may also include virus protection.

Set it up to run automatically daily or weekly, depending on your needs. Take the time to notice results and get rid of anything found. Keep it running constantly while the computer is on and keep your definitions up to date.

In reality that is all you need to do to keep your computer safe from adware and spyware. Of course, being vigilant about the types of websites you visit also helps.

When you realize what is available to you and you can make the best possible decision about the spyware and adware that you are purchase, you can be safe and you can find the internet something beneficial and not a risky thing at all.

www.ingramcontent.com/pod-product-compliance
Lightning Source LLC
Chambersburg PA
CBHW061016050326

40689CB00012B/2663